LIVE A BALANCED LIFE

The "SMPF" Way

SPIRITUAL
MENTAL
PHYSICAL
FINANCIAL

Timothy Trammer I & Timothy Trammer II

Copyright © 2023 Timothy Trammer I & Timothy Trammer II

Scripture quotations marked "KJV" are taken from the Holy Bible, KING JAMES VERSION (Public Domain). Scriptures marked NIV are taken from the NEW INTERNATIONAL VERSION (NIV): Scripture taken from THE HOLY BIBLE, NEW INTERNATIONAL VERSION ®. Copyright© 1973, 1978, 1984, 2011 by Biblica, Inc.™. Used by permission of Zondervan. Scripture quotations marked "NKJV" are taken from the NEW KING JAMES VERSION. Copyright © 1982 by Thomas Nelson, Inc. Used by permission. All rights reserved. No part of this document may be reproduced or transmitted in any form or by any means, electronic, mechanical, photocopying, recording, or otherwise, without prior written permission of the author.

LIVE A BALANCED LIFE
The "SMPF" Way

Timothy Trammer I & Timothy Trammer II
big4foreversmpf.com

ISBN 978-1-949826-60-9
Printed in the USA.
All rights reserved

Published by: EAGLES GLOBAL BOOKS | Frisco, Texas
In conjunction with the 2023 Eagles Authors Course
Cover & interior designed by:
Destined To Publish | www.DestinedToPublish.com

DEDICATION

This book is dedicated to the women in our lives: Samantha Trammer, Dorothy Little, and Joan Williams.

To every seeker of balance and fulfillment, may this book serve as a beacon of light on your journey. To our families, who have been our unwavering source of inspiration and love, this book is dedicated to you. And finally, to each other, in recognition of the bond that has fueled this unique collaboration—father and son, forever united in purpose and passion.

FOREWORD

In an era where our lives are increasingly fast-paced, where technology invades every moment of our existence, and where we are perpetually pushed to accomplish more, achieving balance seems almost like a massive challenge. Live a Balanced Life: The "SMPF" Way: A Dual Perspective on Living Harmoniously is a radiant testament to such a journey, forged by two intertwined lives—the experienced and sage father, Timothy Trammer I, and his impassioned and insightful son, Timothy Trammer II. They invite us to voyage through their minds as they explore and analyze the very essence of a balanced life from their unique vantage points.

This captivating journey has been penned down over two years of deep conversations, shared experiences, and countless hours of reflection. The bond between Timothy Trammer I and Timothy Trammer II, both intense and caring, is a strong undercurrent that flows steadily throughout the book, binding the chapters

FOREWORD

together in a beautiful harmony of wisdom and discovery. Their collaboration is a touching reminder of the precious and dynamic connection between a father and son, symbolizing a bond that is both unique and universal.

Timothy Trammer I, the seasoned father, is a man who has walked the path of life, tasted its bitterness and sweetness, and emerged with a sense of quiet wisdom. His perspective is shaped by a life well lived, marked by triumphs and trials, joys and sorrows. His voice throughout this book is like a guiding beacon—steady, calm, and filled with nuanced understanding of life's complexities.

On the other hand, Timothy Trammer II, the son in his early twenties, brings a fresh, vibrant perspective. His thoughts are inspired with the earnest curiosity of youth, keen observation, and a steadfast pursuit for balance amid the ever-accelerating pace of life. His exploration of balance reflects the nuances of a generation trying to navigate through the pressures of contemporary life while seeking a sense of fulfillment and harmony.

Living a Balanced Life: The "SMPF" Way is a dual perspective on living harmoniously. This book is more than a conventional self-help guide. It's a mirror reflecting the authors' journey in pursuit of equilibrium, a map charting their path, and an open invitation for readers to embark on their own journey towards achieving balance in life. The collaborative voice of this father-son duo transcends age, background, and experience, bridging gaps and uniting perspectives. It is a vivid mix of wisdom and youth, experience and exploration, realism and idealism.

As you dive into the pages of this remarkable collaboration, you will find yourself absorbed in the dance of two generations gracefully intertwining. It is a rare blend of wisdom and vigor,

FOREWORD

experience and innovation, the traditional and the contemporary. Through their shared journey, Timothy Trammer I and Timothy Trammer II demonstrate that balance is not a destination, but rather a process of understanding, adaptation, and growth.

This book holds a magnifying glass to the concept of a balanced life, enriching it with the depth of a father's wisdom and the freshness of a son's perspective. It is their hope, and mine, that through the journey of reading this book, you may find your own path to balance illuminated, and be inspired to embark on your own voyage of harmonious living.

Welcome to a journey that transcends generations. Welcome to Living a Balanced Life: The "SMPF" Way.

Antonique Smith

ACCLAIMED BROADWAY,
FILM AND TELEVISION ACTOR
GRAMMY-NOMINATED ARTIST AND SONGWRITER

TABLE OF CONTENTS

Introduction xi

Chapter 1: "Balance Is Essential" 1

Chapter 2: "Created in His Image" 13

Chapter 3: "Mastering Your Mind" 26

Chapter 4: "Health Is Wealth" 37

Chapter 5: "The Temple" 46

Chapter 6: "The Haves and the Have-Nots" 55

Chapter 7: "Don't Let Your Money $top" 63

INTRODUCTION

If you are holding this book in your hands, it's not a coincidence. This book was designed especially for you. This book is co-authored by a dynamic father and son duo, Timothy Trammer I and Timothy Trammer II. We wrote this after becoming aware of ourselves and our surroundings and noticing that the majority of society is living a life of uncertainty and no direction, which leads to an unbalanced life. This is a book on how to live a balanced life full of love, peace, and prosperity through the four essential areas in everyone's life. What are these four essential areas, you may ask? They are **Spiritual, Mental, Physical, and Financial (SMPF)**.

The first essential area to living a balanced life is Spiritual. It's imperative that each of us get in tune with ourselves and have a relationship with our Creator. In order to reach the greatest version of you, you must have a connection with the Creator of all things, who has the blueprint for your destination. In order

INTRODUCTION

to find your purpose and fulfill it, you must be connected to the Creator.

The second essential area to living a balanced life is Mental. The only person who has absolute control of the mind is the man in the mirror. "As you thinketh, so you are." What you continuously plant into your mind will eventually shape your destiny. That's why it's critical that we guard our mind and be mindful of what we consume mentally.

The third essential area to living a balanced life is Physical. Our body is a temple, and every temple is designed strategically. To operate at our highest level, we must continuously nourish, nurture, and sustain healthy habits that ensure a healthy lifestyle.

The fourth and final essential area of living a balanced life is Financial. Finances are a key component of the lifestyle that you live. Life is what everyone has; style is how you live it. Your economic status is largely based upon your sources of income and investments. Are you living a P.O.O.R. lifestyle—Passing On Opportunities Repeatedly?

In this book, we will reveal various ways to live a balanced life full of love, peace and prosperity, the "SMPF" Way.

1
"BALANCE IS ESSENTIAL"

Living a balanced life means taking care of all aspects of your well-being, most importantly taking care of yourself spiritually, mentally, physically, and financially. These areas are all interconnected, and neglecting any one of them can lead to imbalances in your life. As our awareness of self and our surroundings increased, it led us to realize the significance of balance, which the masses lack severely.

If you don't have balance in life, it can lead to all sorts of problems like feeling depressed or stressed, getting burned out, dealing with anxiety, or even becoming physically sick. Think of it like this: if all you do is concentrate on your job or your money-making pursuits, you might forget to look after your body by not getting the right amount of sleep or doing enough physical activities. On the other hand, if you only focus on your relationships and forget about your personal growth, you could end up feeling unsatisfied or bitter as time goes on. To have a balanced life means that everything in your life works together in harmony. This requires you to really take care of yourself and be aware of your needs, and to make thoughtful decisions about how you use your time, how you spend your energy, and where your money goes.

The month of March in the year 2020 was a big turning point for us, Timothy Trammer I and Timothy Trammer II. As Covid-19 swept across the world causing chaos and confusion, we both had an awakening. We understood that we had to take control of our lives. This was about not just talking about changes, but actually making them. We decided to focus on our personal well-being, our happiness, and understanding who we were, despite the challenges the world was facing due to the pandemic. This was the moment when the idea of a father-son team really took hold.

We began learning, working out, and investing our money together. This shared journey inspired both of us to put in more effort and work smarter, not just for ourselves, but for each other. It turned out to be the perfect partnership at just the right time. As we started examining our lives more closely, we made a decision to dedicate the rest of our lives to becoming the best we could be. In order to become the best versions of ourselves, we realized we needed to focus on four key areas. We call these the Big Four: Spiritual, Mental, Physical, and Financial, or SMPF.

When it comes to the spiritual aspect, we are learning more about our true selves, our natural talents, and our inner powers. We're also strengthening our connection to God, who we know has the master plan for our lives. On the mental front, we're working hard to gain mastery over our minds, striving to become the most intelligent versions of ourselves we can be. Physically, we're committed to fitness and health. We want to become the strongest and healthiest versions of ourselves, to live long and vibrant lives. Finally, on the financial side, we are aiming to make our money work for us, building wealth that we can pass down to our children and grandchildren. We also want to teach and show others how they can do the same. This transformation journey began in a time of global chaos, but it has become our path to personal empowerment, well-being, and true success.

As we are steadily balancing, progressing, and developing ourselves spiritually, mentally, physically, and financially (SMPF), we have a clear-cut vision to share as we pass on our intellectual property, with the result of being of service to anyone seeking a balanced life and wanting to become the best version of themselves. We're committed to sharing what we've learned with others. We want to help anyone who's looking for a more balanced life and those who are seeking to develop themselves. As you develop and become a more well-rounded person, you naturally build stronger connections with people. You become better at understanding others, communicating effectively, and offering support, which leads to better relationships with friends, family, and associates. By becoming the greatest version of yourself, you inspire others to do the same. Your dedication to growth and self-improvement can motivate those around you to seek personal growth and make a positive impact on their own lives. Becoming the best version of yourself allows you to create a lasting legacy. Your achievements, values, and impact on others will be remembered and celebrated, inspiring future generations to strive for greatness as well. We all owe it to God, our family, our loved ones, and ourselves to do all that we possibly can to become the best version of ourselves. Settling for a dull, mediocre, ordinary life may be comfortable and completely normal; however, the rewards of stepping out of your comfort zone and putting forth continuous effort to better yourself are immeasurable and priceless.

In the long term, settling for a life that is less than one's true potential can lead to a sense of stagnation, no fulfillment, and a lack of purpose. People who settle may look back on their lives and wonder what could have been, feeling like they missed out on opportunities for growth and self-discovery. One of the biggest regrets anyone will ever have is sitting down to contemplate their life and seeing that they had the opportunities and potential to accomplish miraculous things but didn't have the courage to follow through—or even coming face to face with someone who is living the life they always dreamed of but didn't have the faith or the work ethic to make happen.

Personal development is a journey that lasts a lifetime. As we actively strive to improve ourselves in every possible way, we understand that fostering self-awareness, making personal growth a priority, and setting clear values and goals are the keys to anyone seeking a balanced life. It doesn't matter where you stand in life at the moment. You have the power to transform your life—to rise from weakness to strength, to turn financial struggle into prosperity, to shift from a state of depression to a state of happiness. Your present circumstances do not define your final destination in life. The critical step is deciding, with firm resolve, to invest your time, energy, and money into evolving into the person you aspire to be. Remember, the power to change and evolve lies within you. It's never too late to embark on this journey of personal growth, to create a life that's fulfilling, balanced, and filled with joy. With dedication and a commitment to self-improvement, you can become the best version of yourself. Life can always be improved upon; every moment provides a chance for renewal, growth, and change.

The importance of carefully choosing where and how to allocate your time, energy, and money cannot be overstated, even though it's often underestimated. We use the word "invest" when talking about time, energy, and money because we should anticipate significant returns from the things we dedicate these resources to. It's essential to remember that each moment that passes is one we will never regain. The situation you find yourself in at this very instant is largely a reflection of how you spent your time, directed your energy, and managed your money a few years prior. Looking ahead, your circumstances a few years from now will be shaped by how you choose to invest these valuable resources today. Therefore, every decision you make about how to use your time, where to put your energy, and when to spend your money matters significantly. Treat these resources as precious investments, and your future self will reap the rewards. In this way, you become an active architect of your own life, building towards a future that reflects your true values and aspirations.

We'd like to introduce the "SMPF" checkpoint. Before you engage in any activities, pose this question to yourself: Is this bringing meaningful value to my life spiritually, mentally, physically, and financially? If the answer is "yes," then by all means, proceed, because it's a wise investment of your resources. On the other hand, if the activity doesn't contribute value, it's crucial to have the self-discipline and boundaries to step back and not engage. This process involves setting clear priorities and making deliberate decisions about how we distribute our time, energy, and money. (We'll dive deeper into the effective allocation of these three resources in subsequent chapters.)

Striving for balance may necessitate that you make tough decisions and set limits that could be uncomfortable in the moment. However, such choices lead to more profound fulfillment and well-being in the long run. They shape your life in a way that aligns with your true values, leading to a healthier, more balanced existence. It's about making choices today that your future self will thank you for. The key lies in understanding that each decision we make—every moment we choose to invest—can propel us further along our journey to personal growth and fulfillment.

We all are aware that success comes with a price, and it's not cheap, no matter what you want to be or achieve. In a world that always seems to want more of our time, finding a balance between work and personal life can be tough, especially for people who are very successful in their work. Consider it like a seesaw. On one side, you have all your work responsibilities, and on the other side, you have your personal life. The trick is to get the seesaw to balance. It's like trying to keep all the plates spinning at once. You might be beyond skilled at your work, but you also want to have time for yourself, your family, and your hobbies. It can feel like a tightrope walk, where you're constantly trying to stay balanced without falling off on either side. What's more, the higher you climb up the ladder of success, the harder it can become to keep everything in balance. Your job or business may demand more of your time and energy, leaving less for the rest of your life. It's a challenge that many successful people face, but it's not impossible to overcome. With careful planning, clear boundaries, and a commitment to taking care of yourself, you can create a life that balances work success with personal fulfillment. Remember, the key is not to let your success in your job overshadow the rest of your life. After all, true success is not just about what you achieve at work, but also about enjoying a well-rounded, fulfilling life.

The Story of Benjamin

Once upon a time, in the bustling city of Metropolis, there lived a wealthy and successful individual named Benjamin Sterling. Benjamin was known far and wide for his extraordinary business acumen and his seemingly unstoppable drive to accumulate wealth. His days were consumed by high-stakes deals, power meetings, and a relentless pursuit of success.

But as the years went by, Benjamin started to feel an emptiness gnawing at his soul. Despite his vast fortune and professional accomplishments, he couldn't shake off the feeling that something was missing from his life. The endless pursuit of wealth had left him isolated, disconnected from his family and friends, and devoid of any real joy.

One fateful evening, as Benjamin stood alone on the balcony of his luxurious penthouse overlooking the glittering city skyline, a sense of longing washed over him. He yearned for balance, for a life that went beyond material possessions and superficial achievements. He yearned for meaning and fulfillment. Driven by this newfound desire, Benjamin embarked on a journey of self-discovery. He sought out wise mentors, read countless books on personal growth, and explored various spiritual practices.

Along the way, he learned the importance of nurturing not just his financial wealth but also his emotional, mental, physical, and spiritual well-being.

With a renewed sense of purpose, Benjamin began to make changes in his life. He started by carving out time for self-care, prioritizing exercise and healthy eating to rejuvenate his physical body. He hired a personal trainer and discovered the joy of outdoor activities like hiking and cycling, reconnecting with nature's beauty.

Realizing the value of human connection, Benjamin mended broken relationships and sought to deepen his bond with his loved ones. He spent quality time with his children, taking them on adventures and cherishing the moments of laughter and love. He rekindled friendships, hosting intimate gatherings to reconnect with old friends and forge new connections.

As his journey progressed, Benjamin also recognized the importance of giving back to society. He established charitable foundations, supporting causes close to his heart, and actively participated in community initiatives. Through his philanthropic endeavors, he discovered the immense joy of making a positive impact on others' lives, beyond the realm of wealth and success.

With each step, Benjamin found himself inching closer to the elusive balance he sought. His days became a delicate dance between business pursuits and personal growth, between financial success and nurturing his well-being. He surrounded himself with like-minded individuals who shared his vision, forming a supportive network of individuals striving for both prosperity and harmony.

"BALANCE IS ESSENTIAL"

As the years rolled on, Benjamin's wealth continued to grow, but it no longer defined him. He had discovered the true essence of a balanced life—a life where material abundance coexisted harmoniously with emotional well-being, vibrant relationships, and a sense of purpose.

People marveled at the transformation they witnessed in Benjamin Sterling. He had become an inspiration, not just as a successful entrepreneur, but also as a beacon of balance and fulfillment. His story touched the hearts of many, reminding them that true wealth lies not merely in financial riches but in an abundance of joy, love, and personal growth.

And so, Benjamin's legacy lived on, not just in the empire he had built but also in the lives he had touched and the example he had set. His journey had taught him that the pursuit of balance was not an endpoint but an ongoing adventure—a dance between ambition and contentment, between worldly success and inner peace.

And as Benjamin looked out over the city, his heart swelled with gratitude. He had found what he had been searching for all along—a life of true abundance, where wealth and balance walked hand in hand, forever intertwined in the tapestry of his existence.

* * *

By prioritizing self-care, self-awareness, and conscious decision-making, you, like Benjamin, can create harmony in all areas of your life and achieve a greater sense of balance and overall prosperity.

According to our perspective, self-care and self-awareness are integrated—or, in other words, they play a role in each other's success. In order to properly care for ourselves, we must be aware of who we are, and awareness is increased by practicing self-care. Self-awareness refers to understanding and recognizing one's own emotions, thoughts, behaviors, and motivations. This ability to accurately assess and monitor one's own feelings and thoughts is crucial for making well-informed decisions, maintaining healthy relationships, and achieving personal goals.

Self-care, on the other hand, involves taking the time to nurture and maintain one's physical, emotional, mental, and spiritual well-being. It includes engaging in activities that promote relaxation, improve health, and foster a sense of balance in life. Engaging in self-care activities, such as mindfulness meditation, journaling, and stretching and training, will enhance self-awareness by encouraging you to reflect on your thoughts, emotions, and bodily sensations.

Being self-aware enables you to identify your needs and recognize when you need to invest more time seeking within. For example, a person who is aware of their own emotional state can take appropriate steps to address it, such as engaging in relaxing activities or seeking social support from family or other trusted individuals in their life.

As you become more self-aware and better at practicing self-care, you are more likely to develop resilience. Resilience is the ability to bounce back from adversity; to cope with and adapt to difficult situations; and to recover quickly from setbacks, challenges, and stress. It involves the capacity to persevere through tough times, to maintain a positive outlook, and to keep moving forward in the face of obstacles.

Understanding one's own emotions, thoughts, and behaviors can lead to better communication, more empathy, and stronger connection in relationships. Additionally, self-care can help prevent fatigue, which can have a negative impact on relationships and your work.

Self-care and self-awareness play an essential role in one's overall well-being, personal growth, and relationship quality. By focusing on both aspects, you can promote a deeper understanding of yourself and better address your needs for a more positive, balanced, and fulfilling life.

Every day we wake up, we are given two precious things: a chance and a choice. It's up to us to live with the choices we make once we've been given a chance. Each new day brings its own set of challenges, obstacles, and opportunities. How we approach life will shape how life responds to us. Or, as Earl Nightingale said it, "Our attitudes towards life will determine life's attitude towards us."

In light of this, we (Timothy Trammer I and Timothy Trammer II) make a conscious decision every day to progress toward becoming the best versions of ourselves in all areas of life: spiritually, mentally, physically, and financially (SMPF). Is it possible for anyone to reach their absolute peak? Absolutely not. However, we choose to continuously work on ourselves, not just for our own growth but also for the benefit of our loved ones.

As we create this book, we are actively strategizing for our family brand and business. We come together daily to brainstorm and bring our vision to life. Our vision is to live a balanced life filled with love, peace, and prosperity. We aim to establish networks that promote wholeness in all aspects of life (SMPF). Our goal is to transform minds into beacons of light, spreading positivity and empowerment. Through sharing our intellectual property, our intention is to uplift and empower others on their own self-development journeys.

We believe in the power of knowledge and its ability to positively impact lives once it has been implemented. By sharing our insights and experiences, we hope to inspire others to embark on their own paths of growth and transformation. We understand that self-development is a lifelong journey, and we are committed to continuously evolving and expanding our own potential. Our aim is to create a ripple effect of positive change, helping individuals unlock their inner potential and live lives of fulfillment and purpose.

Together, we strive to make a difference in the lives of others, contributing to a world where personal growth and empowerment are celebrated and embraced. We invite you to join us on this journey, as we navigate the path of self-development, supporting and uplifting one another along the way.

2
"CREATED IN HIS IMAGE"

When you gaze upon an image of yourself, what thoughts surface in your mind? You might acknowledge your captivating smile or your beautiful eyes, or you might describe yourself as stunning, gorgeous, or handsome. Alternatively, you may find yourself criticizing your appearance, deeming yourself as hideous or fat, or even drawing comparisons to your parents. While these perspectives may feel valid, it's essential to recognize that your true image is a reflection of the Creator of all things. You are God's highest form of creation. As a human being, you hold a distinctive status and divine honor. You are a unique and precious creation, embodying qualities that set you apart in this vast universe. Embrace the beauty and worth that lie within you, for you are an extraordinary and remarkable reflection of the divine.

We live simultaneously on three planes of understanding: we are spiritual creatures, we have an intellect, and we live in physical bodies. But because we lack awareness or understanding of who we are, we're totally locked into a physical world, and we let things outside of us control us. —Bob Proctor

When God made humans, He made us in His own image and likeness. This means that we share certain attributes with God Himself! Two significant traits that we inherit from God are the ability to create and the capacity to love. Sometimes, due to various circumstances in life, it may feel like these characteristics are not innate within us. However, by seeking and connecting with God, we can discover more about our purpose and the inherent powers we possess. Seeking God and establishing a connection with Him can be challenging, especially since we cannot physically see Him. While we can witness His creations in the world around us, such as the sun, moon, oceans, mountains, trees, animals, and even ourselves, it is difficult to grasp the concept without physically seeing the Creator.

Many people require tangible evidence to believe in something. We are reminded every day of God's existence through the beauty and harmony of nature and how everything functions together, yet because we cannot physically see the Creator, it can be hard to fully comprehend this idea. The key is to actively seek Him with a wholehearted approach and an expectation of finding what we are searching for. Life on this earth is short, and time keeps moving forward without waiting for anyone.

We all have an unknown expiration date. It is our sincere wish that no one leaves this earth without having a relationship with the Creator. So, let us seek God sincerely and wholeheartedly, knowing that He has designed us with His attributes. Through this seeking, we can uncover the purpose and power within us, and establish a meaningful connection with the One who created us in His own image and likeness.

We were created to be in a relationship with our Creator. Our worth is connected to our Creator. If God is too great to calculate, then you and I who are made in His image must be of great value too. So, the next time you look at yourself in the mirror, you must understand that your worth is priceless, no matter what you see or what anyone else says. It's imperative to understand how God sees our worth when He looks at us. To realize this, it takes time and continuous effort to seek God and also get in tune with thyself. Seeking God results in getting in tune with yourself, just like a guitar. When a guitar is out of tune, it's just noise that doesn't sound pleasing to the ear, but when it's tuned up, you get a harmonious sound that is pleasing to the ear. Tuning your guitar will optimize your playing, and you will notice when you play a wrong note and be able to correct it. It's the same with life: when you're out of harmony with the Creator, you are just merely existing, but when you're in tune with God and ultimately in tune with yourself, you will discover your true purpose and have a blueprint to fulfill it.

Every single one of us possesses a distinct uniqueness, brimming with gifts, talents, and a purpose waiting to be fulfilled. As the highest form of God's creation, we have been granted dominion and authority to govern the earth with righteousness. Allow that truth to sink deep within you. You are God's ultimate creation. You are adorned with gifts, bestowed with talents, and entrusted with a meaningful purpose. The fact that you are alive and engaged in reading this book is evidence of God's deliberate plan and purpose for your life.

The sooner you become self-aware and attuned to your surroundings, the sooner you can embrace a balanced life infused with love, peace, and prosperity. Open your heart and mind to the understanding that your existence is purposeful and significant. With this awareness, you can step into the fullness of who you are meant to be, living out your unique calling and contributing to the well-being of the world around you.

Self-Control

Timothy Trammer II:

It's the 21st century, and each and every way you look, it seems as if something is trying to grab your attention. We live in a society filled with instant gratification and pleasures. A variety of social media platforms, TV shows, movies, music, and other forms of entertainment are easily accessible due to the advanced technology at the palm of our hands. Temptation is left and right, front and center whether you are searching for it or not. Self-control is the ability to regulate one's emotions, thoughts, and behaviors in the face of temptation and impulses. If we allow our desires to dictate our decisions, our minds and our bodies can quickly spin out of control. I can admit fulfilling certain cravings feels amazing in the moment, but deep down, was it really worth it? We all have some desires and lusts that seem irresistible in the heat of the moment. If we are true to ourselves, we all can name a few habits that we know we shouldn't partake in.

In the pursuit of becoming self-aware and aware of my surroundings, I would waste precious time indulging in activities that didn't help me grow. I was addicted to being under the influence of substances that weren't adding any value to my life spiritually, mentally, physically, or financially. This craving got stronger, slowly but surely, the more I participated in these things. It gave me an instant adrenaline rush, and as time went along, I would have this urge prior to special occasions and social gatherings. I began to realize and acknowledge that this craving was a waste of my valuable time and didn't align with my true identity. In particular, this craving was not progressing me spiritually: it was actually degrading and keeping me farther from my purpose and my Creator. After having that realization, I did my best to stay away from people and places that added fuel to the temptation. I had to submit to the Source and alter my perspective of myself. This transformation didn't happen overnight, and I still sometimes get the urges; however, I continually remind myself of who I am and what my purpose is. As my relationship grew with God through isolating myself, praying daily, and reading my Bible, I soon began to understand that I was born with gifts, talents, and a purpose solely unique to me.

As my relationship with my Creator deepens and evolves, I find that my sense of gratitude and ambition towards life amplifies. I am filled with a profound drive and hunger to demonstrate to God the splendor of His creation by relentlessly striving to tap into my higher self.

This growing connection with my Creator instills within me a profound appreciation for the blessings and opportunities that surround me. I am filled with gratitude for the gift of existence and the countless wonders of the world. This gratitude fuels my desire to make the most of this precious life and to honor the divine spark within me.

With this deepened spiritual bond, my ambitions become aligned with a greater purpose. I am no longer solely driven by personal achievements or external validations. Instead, I am propelled by a profound longing to uncover and embody the limitless potential that lies within me. I strive to reflect the beauty and grace of God's creation through my thoughts, actions, and interactions with others.

In this quest to tap into my higher self, I have embarked on a journey of self-discovery, growth, and self-improvement. I delve into introspection, seeking to understand the depths of my being and to shed light on areas that require healing, transformation, or further development. I am guided by the desire to align my thoughts, beliefs, and behaviors with the divine qualities that reside within me.

This pursuit of tapping into my higher self is not driven by ego or self-aggrandizement, but rather by a genuine yearning to embrace and manifest the essence of love, compassion, kindness, and wisdom that I believe lies within every soul. It is a continuous process of self-reflection, self-awareness, and self-mastery, where I strive to embody the virtues and qualities that reflect the image of my Creator.

As I continue to deepen my connection with my Creator, I become more attuned to the divine guidance that flows through me. I am guided to make choices that align with my highest good and the greater good of all. I am empowered to transcend limitations, overcome obstacles, and embrace the transformative power of growth and evolution.

Ultimately, my journey towards tapping into my higher self is a lifelong pursuit. It is a profound expression of my devotion to the Creator and my reverence for the miracle of life. Through this ongoing journey, I seek to embody the fullest expression of my divine potential and, in doing so, to honor and reflect the beauty of God's creation.

* * *

God's desire is for us to continually seek Him and to show unconditional love to everyone we encounter, no matter what race, religion, or culture you come from. God has revealed His essence to mankind throughout history.

The greatest gift a person can receive is God's one and only Son Jesus Christ as their Lord and Savior. John 3:16 (KJV) is the most memorable scripture that has been quoted throughout the ages: "For God so loved the world, that he gave his only begotten Son, that whosoever believeth in him should not perish, but have everlasting life." The world is missing a key attribute of God, which is love. We have become accustomed to extreme violence and hatred towards one another. Humanity has been in spiritual and physical warfare for quite some time. Innocent blood has been shed since the beginning of time due to power, greed, jealousy, and religion. Not only is hatred being displayed on a global scale, but there is also an absence of love in households, workplaces, and social gatherings. People are being annihilated based upon religion, ethnicity, and just being in the wrong place at the wrong time. As time moves along, you may ask yourself, what's the remedy to cure these issues? The majority of the population is looking for the government to solve these problems; however, the only cure for these adversities is Our Lord and Savior Jesus Christ. Jesus didn't come to condemn the world but to redeem it. With the unconditional love that Jesus Christ has for you and me, we need to mirror that same love when dealing with one another. As Jimi Hendrix said, "When the power of love overcomes the love of power, the world will know peace."

Timothy Trammer I:

Throughout my time on earth, I have observed that when people cross paths in public, they often avoid acknowledging each other. However, I have made it a personal mission to greet and acknowledge individuals when our eyes meet. I have found that a simple phrase like "What's the best part of your day?" can break the ice and create an opportunity for genuine connection. By acknowledging someone's presence, we have the power to shift their attitude and bring positivity into their day.

I vividly remember an experience on a Thursday afternoon while operating our family transportation logistics business with my son. We had a delivery to make at a Walmart pharmacy. As I entered, I encountered an elderly greeter who was diligently working. Curiously, I asked him, "What's the best part of your day?" His response touched me deeply as he shared that no one had ever asked him that before. We engaged in conversation for a few minutes, and at the end, the greeter expressed that I had made his day simply by taking the time to connect with him.

It never ceases to amaze me how a brief encounter with someone can uplift their spirits and bring joy to their soul. By releasing positive energy and showing genuine interest, we express a form of love that aligns with the values God wants us to embody. Each interaction has the potential to make a significant impact, reminding us of the power we hold to brighten someone's day and spread kindness in the world.

Love Is Kind
Timothy Trammer I:

Love is kind. Being kind is a quality of God's unfailing love that you and I must imitate.

Being kind to people has always been in my DNA. I was raised in a household where being kind to others was taught and enforced by my parents. I remember my neighbor Mrs. Buchner, who showed acts of kindness regularly to my family. I remember when my family and I first moved to our new neighborhood, Mrs. Buchner gave us a warm welcome by coming over and introducing herself, and she baked us peanut butter cookies. She also was a gardener and would often bring us fresh tomatoes from her garden. That immediately set the tone for a long-lasting relationship.

A few years later, her husband passed away, and it left her helpless with the things he used to do around the house. To ease some of the stress, I used to help out by cutting Mrs. Buchner's grass, raking her leaves, and shoveling snow, since she was unable to physically do those things. I felt really good afterwards, knowing I had helped someone who was unable to complete those tasks.

The act of kindness that I provided at a young age has carried on into my adulthood. I now make it a habit to serve someone with an act of kindness on a regular basis. One of the ways I show love is when I go through the drive-thru at a restaurant, I pay for the vehicle behind me in addition to my own meal. Once the person behind me gets to the window to pay for his or her food and notices it's already paid for, sometimes they mimic what I did for them and pay for the car behind them. That's an example of paying it forward. Just imagine how the world would be if we made it a habit to show some type of kindness to someone without any strings attached.

I am part of a group of friends who gather once a month in downtown Indianapolis, Indiana, to support the homeless community. Our primary focus is to provide them with food, cater to their personal needs, and, most importantly, share the gospel of Jesus Christ. To ensure the success of our event, we engage in proper planning discussions. We cover various topics such as food and beverages, clothing items, protocols for unpredictable weather, and other necessary resources.

On the scheduled day, we come together at the designated location and set up all the required supplies and equipment. As we prepare, the people we aim to serve are drawn to us, observing our preparations. Before commencing our service to the community, we unite in prayer, seeking guidance and blessing for our endeavors.

Once everything is ready, each of us takes on our assigned roles, and those in need form a single-file line. We distribute food and beverages, allowing individuals to choose the clothing items they require from the selection provided. Additionally, my wife, Samantha, who is a nurse, offers her valuable contribution by checking the blood pressure of those in need. If any abnormal results arise, she ensures they receive appropriate medical attention.

Life is unpredictable, and one never knows when circumstances may lead to a loss of everything, requiring that they rely on the kindness of others to fulfill basic necessities. Our act of compassion is not driven by boasting, pride, or personal gain.

It stems from a genuine love that God has instilled within our hearts. We understand that we are all interconnected and that offering support and care to those in need is an expression of the divine love we have been blessed with.

Patience

Timothy Trammer I:

Maintaining patience is vital for leading a life free from stress. When one practices patience, their mindset remains centered on the positive potential of any given situation, enabling them to remain cool, calm, and collected. Patient individuals are less likely to exhibit anger or intense emotions during times of crisis. Research suggests that patient people often experience reduced levels of depression and negative emotions, as they possess better coping mechanisms for navigating challenging or stressful circumstances.

Patience is not developed overnight; oftentimes, it takes years of practice. I can recall when I served in the military years ago as a drill sergeant, and my job consisted of training newly enlisted civilians on how to become a soldier. They had no idea what it took to become a soldier and how the army functioned as a whole. It was my duty as a drill sergeant for the next eight weeks to teach the newly enlisted civilians about basic training, survival skills, and other tactics. This also included small details such as properly cleaning the barracks and making their beds according to the Standard Operating Procedures (SOP). These soldiers came from all different walks of life. Some of the civilians had never experienced any type of structure or discipline in their homes or received specific methods of instructions consistently. It was a cultural shock for most of them, and it took time for them to adapt to this new way of living. With that being said, it was important for the drill sergeant to maintain authority and implement the act of being patient. It was challenging to be patient at times, since your patience was tested throughout each and every day.

* * *

To speak honestly, patience is a quality that is tested on a daily basis, and this virtue is often lacking in the majority of people. Patience is a crucial element for achieving anything meaningful in life. Whether it's pursuing goals, nurturing relationships, overcoming challenges, or engaging in the process of learning and teaching, patience is required. The key question is whether you can endure and remain patient as you journey through life's trials and tribulations.

Obtaining true patience comes from being mindful of the circumstances at hand. It involves reminding yourself that difficult moments are temporary and will eventually pass. Additionally, seeking guidance and strength from our Lord and Savior can help activate and cultivate patience within you, day by day. By relying on a higher power and practicing mindfulness, you can navigate the tests of patience that arise in your life and maintain a steady and resilient attitude.

"Be completely humble and gentle; be patient, bearing with one another in love." —Ephesians 4:2 (NIV)

"CREATED IN HIS IMAGE"

We resemble the Creator of all things! We mirror God's attributes, and we must be connected to the Source not only to realize His powers and intelligence but also to realize and activate the powers and intelligence that He instilled in us. Show love to your loved ones; show love to those who you encounter once and may never encounter again.

Remember, you are created in His image.

3
"MASTERING YOUR MIND"

"The human mind is the last great unexplored continent on the earth. It contains riches beyond our wildest dreams, and it will return anything we want to plant."

—*Earl Nightingale*

If you lack control over your own mind, you become like a feather being carried by the winds of life. The truth is, your mind is the only aspect you have the power to govern. You cannot control the weather, other people, or anything external. The only realm of influence you possess lies within your own thoughts. Without control over your mind, you journey through life with no authority, no impact. You are unable to steer any aspect of your existence. You become a mere feather, carried aimlessly by life's gusts, shifting from happiness to sadness without agency. You rely solely on the hope that fortune will befall you, leaving you vulnerable and defenseless when confronted with genuine pain or tragedy.

We have been given a profound gift from our Creator, which is our mind. Our mind has two parts: the conscious mind and the subconscious mind. The conscious mind is what we're aware of right now—ourselves and the world around us. It's about what we're thinking about at the moment. The subconscious mind, on the other hand, absorbs everything we frequently think or experience. It doesn't question or argue like the conscious mind does. It just takes in everything, good or bad, that comes through our senses: touch, taste, smell, sight, and hearing.

Our subconscious mind is like a memory bank. It keeps a record of all our experiences and ideas, even after we've forgotten them. Some people call the subconscious mind an "autopilot" because it's so much more powerful than the conscious mind and controls much of our lives. It takes care of things like breathing, digesting food, and keeping our hearts beating. And it does all this without us having to think about it, which is a good thing. It's always at work, guiding our usual emotions and habits. The more often we do something, the more likely our subconscious mind is to remember it.

Think of our subconscious mind like a computer. The computer stores any data you feed it, be it positive or negative. But over time, the computer can get viruses from infected files or websites. These viruses can spread and cause problems. Similarly, if we constantly expose ourselves to negative thoughts or influences, we can also "catch a virus" of negativity. This can happen based on the people we often meet, the things we regularly listen to or watch, and the words we frequently tell ourselves.

"MASTERING YOUR MIND"

Timothy Trammer I:

We all want the best for our family members—especially the two that gave birth to us. Yet an individual's repetitive thoughts and words can lead to undesirable consequences. I recall how my mother often claimed she was "broke," even when she had sufficient funds and was not in need of anything. I advised her against using the term "broke," as it was sending out negative energy and embedding an unwelcome "virus" in her subconscious mind. The subconscious mind doesn't evaluate or rationalize; it simply accepts the information given as truth, regardless of its accuracy. It might be a common phrase people use to avoid lending money, or perhaps it's a statement that's been ingrained in their subconscious mind over the years. Eventually, the words she frequently uttered took root in her subconscious and manifested as her reality.

When I was deeply involved in the sport I love, basketball, I developed a daily habit of speaking positive affirmations out loud that were specifically related to basketball. I understood the power of spoken words and their ability to either motivate and uplift or tear down and defeat. My goal was to become the greatest shooter in the history of basketball, so I began affirming, "I am the number one shooter in the world." I declared myself the best jumpshot shooter on the planet, surpassing even those in the prestigious National Basketball Association (NBA). As I consistently voiced these positive affirmations, I started to truly believe in what I was saying. In my mind, no one could convince me that there existed a better shooter than myself. While I had always been a skilled shooter, once I ingrained the words "I am the number one shooter in the world" into my subconscious mind, my shooting abilities reached exceptional levels. Whether I was practicing, playing a pickup game, or in an official match, I carried the unwavering belief that I was the best shooter in the world. As I mentioned earlier, whatever we consistently feed our subconscious mind, it accepts as truth, regardless of whether it is objectively true or not. My thoughts became my reality, and this mindset opened up numerous opportunities for me to showcase my exceptional shooting skills.

In 2018, I was going through a rough time in my life physically where my blood pressure got out of hand. I had been taking blood pressure medication for over 20 years, and I made a conscious decision to stop taking it and to replace it with all natural supplements. I didn't know that you shouldn't suddenly stop taking your blood pressure medication without the doctor's approval. This took place while my wife and children were out of town and I had stayed back at home. Three days off from taking my blood pressure medication, I felt myself getting dizzy and my heart began to race. I immediately began taking deep breaths to try to get my heart rate back to normal.

After 10 minutes had gone by, it felt like my heart was about to explode. I was contemplating calling an ambulance, but I decided not to. Another 10 minutes passed by, and my heart rate still hadn't come back to its original configuration, so I called 911 for help. When the ambulance arrived, I expressed what I was currently experiencing, and they immediately checked my blood pressure, which was 210 over 110. If you didn't know, that's considered stroke level. I was then rushed to the emergency room. The doctor put me on a IV and a different medication to attempt to get my blood pressure back down.

"MASTERING YOUR MIND"

While I was resting in the room I was placed in, my three sisters and brother-in-law were notified by my neighbor that I was in the emergency room. My neighbor asked my wife, Samantha, "Was everything okay?" Samantha clearly was clueless due to being out of town, and then my neighbor said that they saw me being transported by the ambulance. So she called my sisters to see if they could find out what was going on. My sisters asked what was going on with me, and I expressed to them that I had stopped taking my blood pressure medication in favor of natural supplements. My sister Regina stated, "You should never take yourself off of blood pressure medication without the doctor's approval." I responded, "Now I know that was the wrong thing to do." I told my sisters to get in contact with Samantha and let her know that I was okay and the doctor was just waiting on my blood pressure to come down before releasing me. After several hours, my blood pressure finally dropped back to normal, and I was released with two new blood pressure pills.

A week after being released from the hospital, I noticed that my body had started to feel different. I was experiencing a lot of side effects from the new blood pressure pills. I got to the point where it was hard to walk down the steps without being out of breath and feeling my heart pounding. After doing research on both medications, I found that one of the medications was giving me all of the side effects, so I let my wife know. I had gone to a dark place: I was depressed and stressed, and anxiety was setting in. I even stopped driving because every time I got on the road, I would have a panic attack and look for the nearest hospital or fire station. My mind started playing tricks on me, and for the next six to eight months, I thought I was going to die on a daily basis. I had come to the point where I didn't want to be left alone at home. I used to hate seeing my wife go to work because I knew I would start to have panic attacks. I never told my family exactly what I was going through, because I didn't want them to worry about me. Each day, I felt myself getting worse and worse.

Without consulting my primary physician, I decided to stop taking one of the blood pressure medications I had been prescribed. Deep down, I knew that was a major risk based upon what I had previously experienced; however, I was tired of experiencing the side effects. I finally told my physician that I had stopped taking the medication that was giving me the side effects. He was okay with it since my blood pressure was stable. Even though my blood pressure was stable, my subconscious mind still reminded me of the panic attacks and the anxiety.

I said to myself that I could no longer live in fear. I remembered the verse 2 Timothy 1:7—"God didn't give us the spirit of fear but of power, love and a sound mind." I started speaking this verse into my life all throughout each day until it got embedded in me and became my reality. I began to meditate and listen to uplifting, inspirational speeches. The more I spoke positive, powerful affirmations over my life, the more I began to feel better and regain confidence in myself. As my mentality got stronger, my physical body was regaining its strength as well. Negative thoughts about my recent past experiences would try to creep in, but I would immediately combat them with positive affirmations and meaningful thoughts of the powerful man God created me to be. This rough patch in my life ultimately helps remind me of the power of the mind, whether used for my benefit or detriment.

"MASTERING YOUR MIND"

"Whatever we plant in our subconscious mind and nourish with repetition and emotion will one day become a reality." — Earl Nightingale

The Power of the Mind

"While human beings can speak at a rate of 150 to 200 words per minute, and we read from 200 to 400 words per minute on average, we think at the rate of 1300 to 1800 words per minute."

—Glenn Davis

Timothy Trammer II:

Before I had the information about how powerful my mind was, I would allow my mind to run rapidly with random thoughts that I shouldn't have been thinking. I used to dwell on the past and be anxious about future events. This led to me continuously thinking about the worst-case scenario in these situations. Constantly thinking about negative past memories and overthinking upcoming events is a total energy drainer and confidence killer.

One day I was on my iPhone, and I noticed an app called "Books," which is automatically installed on every Apple device. It is filled with audiobooks and ebooks so you can either listen or read directly from your device. I didn't have anything in particular that I was searching for; I just went to "top free books" under the "Health, Mind & Body" category. I was scrolling and scrolling, and I came across a book titled As a Man Thinketh by James Allen. It was officially published in 1903! What caught my attention

"MASTERING YOUR MIND"

was the introduction, which reads: "Mind is the master power that moulds and makes, and man is mind, and evermore he takes the tool of thought, and, shaping what he wills, brings forth a thousand joys, a thousand ills: He thinks in secret, and it comes to pass: environment is but his looking glass."

After reading that, I definitely knew that it was published in 1903 based upon the phrases and vocabulary that were used; however, when I realized that the book was only 53 pages long, I immediately downloaded it and began reading. This short book completely shifted my mentality and self-awareness. After I read this, I began to analyze my personal life. I quickly came to the realization that my inner self-thoughts and inner self-talk have always correlated with the outer conditions of my life.

I started to study this powerful book, and my goal since I first got hold of it has been to sharpen my mentality as much as possible. I started slowly, with a goal of reading 10 pages of the book every day. As time went along, I purchased the audio version for $3.99, and now I listen to the whole book once a day, which only takes 46 minutes.

I continue to study this tiny book and do my best to make it a daily read, simply because of how powerful the context is and the short amount of time it takes to read. I now have a deep desire to master my mind and spread the knowledge of how anyone can do so. Daily I remind myself that the thoughts that I choose repeatedly are having a huge impact on my life. My inner character and outer circumstances are all connected to the way I view myself and talk to myself. With that being said, I am very cautious of what I allow to come in my mind and what I allow to stay in it. When I say I am cautious, I check whatever has the

"MASTERING YOUR MIND"

attention of my eyes and ears. I ask myself, is this enhancing my mentality? Is this helping me grow? What can I learn from this and share with someone else? I keep these questions in mind when dealing with other people and certain activities.

With this knowledge of how powerful the mind is, I have implemented a few habits to uplift my mentality: uplifting self-talk, visualization of my greatest self, and reading books and listening to speeches about the enhancement of the mind. I noticed that decreasing my consumption of certain entertainment such as music, TV shows, movies, and social media helped clear my mind.

* * *

You can't fall victim to gossip, petty worries, self-pitying, fear and doubt. These are indications of weakness, which lead to failure and unhappiness. Everything isn't always sunshine and rainbows; however, you should make it a habit to find something positive out of every situation. Look at the glass as half full and not half empty. Become an optimist and not a doubter. These small alterations in your character will help make your life more enjoyable, and people want to be in the presence of positive, high-energy individuals.

Developing your mind into a beacon of light is not easy, especially if you have been programmed to do the opposite. However, you must practice and put forth continuous effort day by day—you will soon see the rapid transformation of your inner self, and the outside conditions of your life will harmonize with it. It's inevitable! Positive, powerful thoughts of love, peace, and prosperity can only produce love, peace, and prosperity, while on the other hand, thoughts of sickness, disease, hatred, envy, and lack will only produce negative and depressing circumstances. A physically weak person can make themselves strong through the repetition of physical training, and the same is true for the mentally weak person: they can make themselves mentally strong by training their mind.

Whether you are aware of it or not, your mentality has shaped you into the person you are today and will play a role in the person you are becoming. Let me repeat that. Whether you are aware of it or not, your mentality has shaped you into the person you are today and will play a role in the person you are becoming. Now that you are aware of this power within you, who are you going to become? What thoughts are you going to continuously let sit in your mind and grow? Uplift your thoughts and you will uplift your life.

It is imperative that we guard our thoughts and do our best to eliminate thoughts that don't align with who we desire to be and where we desire to go. Your ears, mouth, and eyes are the gateways to the mind. Be extremely careful of what you consume through your ears and eyes, because if it is consumed enough, it will come out of your mouth. And what you speak into the atmosphere is just as powerful as what you think. However, the power of the mind and the tongue in unison is extremely supernatural, especially if used in a purposeful and intentional way. Repeating uplifting and encouraging affirmations to yourself over and over throughout the day is a habit that we highly recommend for everyone!

Society is subconsciously interested in you conforming—conforming to mediocrity and limited beliefs. From birth, we are being programmed to think and act a certain way based upon who we are surrounded by. If we don't learn how to think for ourselves, we will always be in a position where we rely on others to think and make decisions for us. It is easy and completely normal nowadays to be conformed to the world. Thinking like, behaving like, and blending in with the masses only gets you the same results as the masses. And that's totally fine, but those who seek to become the greatest version of themselves must understand this quote by John Maxwell: "How big we think determines the size of our accomplishments."

Method of Instructions:

Renew your mind: Set your mind on things that are positive and take control of your mind. Always feed your mind with powerful affirmations daily. Practice daily meditations and listen to inspirational content/music.

Virus remover: Clean out your subconscious mind that has stored all the negative past experiences. Replace with fruitful, meaningful thoughts.

Guard your mind: Be aware of what you consume mentally, Continue to choose powerful, uplifting thoughts of love, peace, and prosperity.

4
"HEALTH IS WEALTH"

We often undervalue things that are given to us freely, placing greater emphasis on materialistic items we purchase. These tangible possessions, no matter their price, can be replaced, which essentially makes them cheap. In contrast, the truly priceless things in life are inherent to us: our mind, our body, and our soul. The saying "Health Is Wealth" signifies that health is the most precious treasure one can have. The term "asset" is defined as something beneficial or of great worth. As American philosopher Ralph Waldo Emerson penned in 1860, "The first wealth is health," reminding us that no material possession can rival the importance of maintaining good health and well-being.

Our physical bodies are designed strategically. We are incredible organisms, capable of some extraordinary things that would absolutely blow our own minds if we ever truly tapped into ourselves. We must speak life over our bodies through positive, powerful affirmations. Oftentimes I hear people continuously saying out loud, "I am sick," or they keep repeating the diagnosis of what the doctor claims they have, such as "I have cancer," "I have diabetes," "I have COVID-19." Instead of claiming those diagnoses and constantly putting those words in the atmosphere, let's switch up our vocabulary and shout throughout the day, "I am healed." "There is no sickness or disease in my body." "I am healthy." "My body is clean, my bloodstream is clean, my mind is clean." We must make it a habit to speak life over our lives. Proverbs 18:21 (NIV) says, "The tongue has the power of life and death, and those who love it will eat its fruit." This verse carries a powerful message about the influence and consequences of our words.

The phrase "The tongue has the power of life and death" suggests that our words can either build up or destroy. Positive, encouraging words can inspire, motivate, and bring joy, while negative words can cause harm, breed negativity, and lead to destruction. This highlights the importance of carefully choosing our words, as they have the potential to create or devastate.

"And those who love it will eat its fruit" suggests that people will experience the consequences of their words. If someone speaks positively and constructively, they will enjoy beneficial results (the "fruit"). Conversely, if they use their words carelessly or harmfully, they may face negative outcomes. In a nutshell, this verse emphasizes the significant impact of our words on ourselves and others, and urges us to use them wisely and kindly.

Life is about trying to keep death as far away as possible. Would life exist if there was no death? Sometimes, it feels like death is trying to show up too soon, and we have to do everything we can to live longer. Illness tries to limit our health, but we need to do all we can to stay healthy and keep illness away. Life can be tough, throwing big challenges at us. But if we don't get good at handling the small challenges first, we'll have a hard time dealing with the bigger ones.

So, in simple terms, life is like a constant game where we try to stay ahead. It's like a tug-of-war with death and illness, where we're always pulling on the rope of good health and longevity. It's not an easy game, but it's one we all play. Just like in any game, we need to master the basic moves before we can tackle the tougher ones. In life, this means learning to overcome small challenges before we're ready to face the bigger ones. The more we practice, the better we get, and the more prepared we are for whatever life throws at us.

Good health is essential to creating wealth or any other worthwhile accomplishment. To fulfill your purpose in life, live your life to the fullest, and achieve your dreams and goals, it's vital to be healthy. As you begin to live in a healthy state physically and mentally, you will have more energy, and your overall attitude will be optimistic and excited about the future. You will become more efficient, achieving maximum productivity with minimum wasted effort. The goals you have set for yourself are much simpler to accomplish once you are physically and mentally healthy. As you begin to fulfill these goals that you have set for yourself, your self-assurance will rise, and your dreams that previously looked too difficult to achieve will become attainable, especially as your mentality grows.

Having trustworthy relationships with family and other loved ones is one of life's greatest accolades. When we are in a healthy state mentally and physically, there is much joy in socializing and spending quality time with others.

Living a health-conscious lifestyle and becoming someone who knows their worth and values themselves will ultimately have more accolades in life than those who aren't health-conscious. People who are always under the weather and ill generally aren't as proactive as healthy people. When you are sick, you require more time off to rest, recover, heal, and sleep, and you may have days where you just can't get out of bed. That's fine on occasion when you have a common cold, flu, or any other ailment; however, people who are generally in good shape are way more prolific and productive. When you are living a balanced life health-wise, you'll be able to take charge of every aspect of your day-to-day life.

Timothy Trammer II:

Besides a few common colds and other viruses, my physical body has been healthy and athletic for my entire existence. I'm beyond grateful and happy to say that I haven't experienced or been faced with any major sickness, disease, or disability throughout my life. With that being said, when I'm under the weather and not feeling my best, it's extremely difficult to function, and I know for a fact that I can't operate at my best. The only thing on my mind in those brief periods of time is that I wish I was feeling better—I wish I was healthy and in my normal state. Then I start to overthink and contemplate what caused me to begin feeling sick in the first place. The feeling of illness and sickness makes me want to isolate myself and not do anything physically or socially. After some time has gone by, I get extremely upset that I'm not feeling my best, and I go into this mode of deep drive and determination to do all that I possibly can to get over the sickness as soon as possible and to never get back in that sick state again.

When I am feeling under the weather, I do my best to distance myself from others so I am not spreading anything. Hot steamy showers and utilizing the sauna at the gym are definitely two of my favorite things to speed my recovery process. Getting as much sunlight and being in nature as much as possible, especially when it's not cold outside, helps boost my mood and energy. I also speak powerful, positive affirmations over my life, such as "I am healed, healthy, and whole," "There is no sickness or disease in my body," "I am healthy and strong," "My body is clean, my bloodstream is clean, my mind is clean," "I'll never be sick another day in my life," "My immune system is strong," "I am filled with strength," and "My body is full of energy." Putting these words into the atmosphere gives me reassurance and confidence that these words will be my reality. Hot steamy showers, utilizing the sauna at the gym, being in nature, soaking up the sun, and speaking powerful affirmations into my life do not only uplift me while I'm not at my best—I have also added these regimens to my day-to-day life due to the positive, healthy results that I am experiencing.

* * *

Being sick, ill, and under the weather certainly makes us all want to isolate ourselves and shut out the world. Each and every person knows someone who is always verbally complaining about aches, pains, and sickness. Nobody wants to be that person.

Sickness and disease cost money. Regardless of your economic status, if you don't have your health, then that is something you will long for. There is abundant proof that money does buy better healthcare. However, money can't buy health. Even if you have exceptional health coverage, there are still expenses associated with ill health and/or disease. Any type of pharmaceutical costs and time away from work will result in a substantial amount of money that you will have to pay out. If you truly desire to live a balanced life full of love, peace, and prosperity, it's imperative that you make a conscious decision to do all that you can to remain in a healthy state. Sickness and injuries, on the other hand, hinder your ability to operate at a high level.

Timothy Trammer I:

Do you know someone who had to take an extended leave of absence from work as a result of sickness or physical injury? Of course we all know someone who has experienced that. I can think of a time when my coworker Maurice tore his Achilles tendon while delivering mail to a residential house. This type of injury kept Maurice out of work for approximately six to eight months. When he did report back to work, he had to go on light duty, which means he could not perform at the high level he did prior to the injury. He remained on light duty for several weeks. Management noticed that he was not capable of fulfilling his assigned task. They gave Maurice a particular time frame to heal and recover so he could perform his duties according to the Standard Operating Procedure (SOP). After the time frame expired, management noticed that he was still unable to fulfill his duties, which led to him getting an extended period of time to be able to function according to the SOP. Once again, he failed, and this resulted in Maurice getting terminated.

"HEALTH IS WEALTH"

This is a real-life example of someone losing their only source of income due to unfortunate circumstances. This put him in a stressful situation, especially because he had a wife and three children to provide for. Too much stress on any individual can lead to other health issues. I kept in touch with Maurice, and soon after he was terminated, he found another job. Maurice told me that he felt as if he was actually stronger and capable of doing more physically than before the injury. He shared with me that while physical therapy helped tremendously, the main key to his rejuvenated body was envisioning himself healthier than ever.

* * *

Imagine you are in top-tier shape physically and mentally and you are on an exotic island with some close friends and family. This exotic island is full of beautiful people from all around the world who made a conscious decision to live a balanced life full of love, peace, and prosperity. Your life is filled with love, peace, and prosperity! You're lying on the beach, soaking up the sun, while the cool breeze keeps you all from overheating. You are observing the tall palm trees, baby blue ocean, and soft sand in between your toes while drinking water from a coconut. Life is wonderful—no worries, no stress, just pure relaxation. You see people racing on jet skis. You see a newlywed couple parasailing in the distance. All of sudden, you hear a familiar sound, and you glance to the right and left to see where the sound is coming from.

You notice a bride being escorted by her father. She is wearing a pure white dress with a long train. The closer the bride gets to the awaiting groom, the more the tears of joy flow from her face. You were so relaxed and in such a state of bliss that you didn't even notice the beach wedding ceremony that was about to take place 20 feet away from you. The wedding guests are all dressed in different shades of blue, sitting in white chairs facing the ocean. As the bride is finally in the presence of the groom, there is a huge round of applause from everyone in sight. This wedding has everyone's attention. People who were walking the shore have stopped and are staring in complete amazement at the unexpected beauty. It seems as if everyone has their phone out recording this special moment, including the professional videographer. You can literally feel the love in the atmosphere, and the love is spreading throughout the beach.

The bride and groom had planned for a small destination wedding ceremony; however, there turned out to be a multitude of onlookers who waited patiently for the start of the ceremony. With all of the healthy vibes circulating throughout the perimeter, the minister receives the nod to start the ceremony. The bride and groom strategically wrote their personal vows, and they spoke them out loud with passion while gazing intently into one another's eyes. Once the vows are completed and the rings are exchanged, the minister says, "I now pronounce you husband and wife. You may kiss your bride." We all know what happens after the wedding ceremony: pictures, reception, and partying all night long.

How do you feel after imagining what you just read? Did you actually envision being on the exotic island and witnessing the wedding ceremony? If so, that's power! Our brain has a difficult time identifying what is just an imagination and what's actually real. In our minds, we can imagine different types of schemes and know how each would play out. With that being said, what you think about or even imagine can affect your health in a positive or negative way. You need to imagine yourself in the most healthy, productive state, living in your dream body. As you continuously imagine yourself as that healthy person, you will soon take action and eventually become what you imagine.

> The body is the servant of the mind. It obeys the operations of the mind, whether they be deliberately chosen or automatically expressed. . . . Disease and health, like circumstances, are rooted in thought. . . . The body is a delicate and plastic instrument, which responds readily to the thoughts by which it is impressed.
>
> —James Allen "As a Man Thinketh"

Methods of Instructions

Speak powerful, positive affirmations into your life about your health.

Imagine yourself in your healthiest state physically, mentally, emotionally.

Take actions that align with your words and thoughts.

5
"THE TEMPLE"

Our body is a temple, and every temple is conceived in detail and for a specific purpose. Treating our bodies as temples is an important concept that can help us live healthier and more fulfilling lives. By acknowledging the intricate design of our bodies and their purpose, we can better understand the significance of living a healthy lifestyle.

The purpose is to honor God by living a healthy lifestyle. We should treat our bodies with high respect and great esteem. Our goal should be to strengthen our body and not destroy it. Our bodies were designed strategically, so they require work to maintain and keep in a good state.

Nourish and Nurture

To honor and respect your physical self, you should focus on nourishing and nurturing your body. Nourishing the body first starts with what you consume. Food is our body's main source of energy and nutrients.

I'm sure we all have heard of the phrase "You are what you eat." Well, this figure of speech implies that the quality of the food we consume plays a crucial role in molding our physical, mental, and emotional health. Basically, if we eat a balanced, nutrient-rich diet, our bodies will function in the best or most favorable way, and we will enjoy better health. In contrast, if we consume unhealthy, nutrient-poor foods, our health is bound to suffer, and we may be more prone to illnesses and diseases. We all should know this by now, but it is clear that we don't always take it into consideration.

This is a friendly reminder that sodas, energy drinks, and sugar-sweetened fruit juices provide no value to our physical body whatsoever. We also must remember that our bodies are made up of more than 60% water. We know you have heard this a million times; however, drink more water! Do yourself a favor and hydrate your beautiful, well-designed temple. This is a necessity for maintaining proper bodily functions such as digestion, absorption, body temperature, and circulation. Guess what: you can also hydrate your body by eating your fruits and vegetables! Watermelon, cucumber, strawberries, cantaloupe, grapefruit, celery, tomatoes, bell peppers, zucchini, spinach—we can go on and on. These may not be your favorite foods taste-wise, but they all contain a great amount of water, and they also provide the body with essential nutrients.

We know that not everyone can grow their own garden with fresh fruits and vegetables, or be a chef or hire a chef; nevertheless, let's do our best to stay away from anything that falls in the categories of fast food or processed food. It is vital to consume a variety of foods that provide the body with essential nutrients such as fiber, minerals, and vitamins. Depending on your health goals, your diet will vary; nonetheless, a balanced diet includes a mix of fruits, vegetables, whole grains, lean proteins, and healthy fats. These foods supply the body with the energy it needs to function properly and help maintain a healthy weight. No, consuming nutrient-poor foods occasionally is not going to harm you immediately. Everything is okay in moderation. However, regularly consuming certain foods that provide none of the essential vitamins, minerals, and nutrients will deteriorate your body over time.

Timothy Trammer II:

Recently, I was in the presence of my wonderful family, and we were socializing, eating, and having a great time. I got carried away with the variety of food choices available. The selection of food that day was wide, and as everything was being prepared, I volunteered myself to be in charge of taste testing to see what the food was lacking or if it was ready to be served. I found myself full before the meal was even fully done. Then, when everything was ready and it was time to eat with everyone, I still loaded up two plates and was eager to dive in. I completely stuffed myself—I ate so much that I could barely move off the couch. I was drinking soda and juice instead of water.

Slowly but surely, I started to feel more sluggish and tired. It was getting late in the evening and it was time for everyone to go their separate ways. I soon realized that I was constipated from overeating and the lack of water in my body; however, I didn't think too much of it, so I went straight to sleep and told myself that I would drink a lot of water as soon as I woke up. I was tossing and turning all night. My stomach was bloated, and around 2:00 a.m., I jumped up out of my bed and ran to the bathroom to throw up all of the food I had eaten! What made everything worse was the fact that some of it didn't make it in the toilet and I had to clean up the mess while still in pain. I'm sure we've all been there before. The rest of the day, my head was throbbing, and I still had a lingering stomachache while feeling nauseated.

This experience reminded me that I must be mindful of what I consume and eat in moderation. I was savoring each bite, for sure; however, I needed to be more aware of my body's fullness instead of continuously eating. Oh, and of course I needed to drink more water, which was a big factor as well. Immediately, once I started to feel back to normal, which was the following day, I decided to go on a fast to discipline myself. Fasting is the voluntary practice of abstaining from food and, in some cases, certain beverages for a specific period of time. It has been practiced for centuries for various reasons, including religious observance, health improvement, and weight loss.

There are different types of fasting, each with its unique approach to food restriction. Two common forms of fasting are intermittent fasting and water fasting. Intermittent fasting involves cycling between periods of eating and fasting, with various methods dictating the length of the fasting window. A popular intermittent fasting method is the 16/8 method, which is fasting for 16 hours and eating within an 8-hour window. Water fasting is a more extreme form of fasting, in which an individual abstains from all food and only consumes water for a specific period of time, typically ranging from 24 hours to several days. I made up my mind that I was going to only drink water for the next 36 hours, which was not an easy task at all. However, the physical and mental benefits were definitely worth the discipline. After my fasting period, my body and mind both felt much clearer and cleaner. If you have never fasted before, we highly recommend you challenge yourself with one of these two forms of fasting.

* * *

Now that we are caught up on what the temple needs to consume on a regular basis, let's bring attention to what the physical body needs to actively participate in on a regular basis. Exercising continuously is an important element for anyone seeking to live a balanced life. Physical training will improve cardiovascular health, increase muscle strength and endurance, and reduce the risk of chronic diseases. Training physically strengthens not only the body but the mind as well. By maintaining a healthy and fit body, you not only improve your physical health but also create a strong foundation for personal and professional success. Pursuing and maintaining physical health requires discipline, commitment, and goal-setting. These skills are transferable to other facets of life and will contribute to overall success.

Regular exercise and maintaining a healthy body weight will lead to increased self-confidence and a positive body image. When you feel good about your appearance, it will boost your self-esteem and help you feel more confident in other areas of your life. Physical activity helps to increase energy levels, improves blood circulation, and decreases fatigue. Higher energy levels can contribute to increased productivity, better focus, and the ability to accomplish more across the board. Developing physically will contribute to increased physical resilience, allowing you to bounce back more easily from injuries or setbacks. This resilience can carry over to mental strength, helping you maintain a positive outlook and persevere through difficult situations such as stress, anxiety, and depression.

People won't respect you if your body, habits, and movements demonstrate that you don't respect yourself. Nobody is going to truly care about your health and happiness like you do, so you must get active and stay active. The idiom "use it or lose it" can be correlated with a lot of different topics; however, it connects perfectly with the utilization of the muscles. If you don't engage in regular physical activity or strength training, your muscles will weaken and decrease in size, a process known as muscle atrophy. This loss can be particularly pronounced as you age, making it even more crucial to maintain an active lifestyle. Incorporating regular exercise into your daily routine can involve enjoyable activities like going for a walk or jog, hopping on your bike for a ride, swimming laps at the pool, hitting the gym to lift weights, practicing calisthenics at home, or joining a sports team with friends. Your physique goals will determine the foods you need to consume and the workouts you should focus on.

Timothy Trammer II:

"It is a shame for a man to grow old without seeing the beauty and strength of which his body is capable." That was said perfectly by Socrates. When I first heard this famous quote in the audio version, it inspired me, and I immediately wrote the statement down for remembrance. Reading that statement is a part of my pre-workout routine. Every time I read it, it instantly boosts my energy and empowers me to conquer all of the challenges I set for myself, which leads to a newfound confidence. I am loving this pursuit towards a healthy physique that cannot be purchased but is only earned through consistency, discipline, passion, and pain.

When I am training, I have this mentality of becoming the healthiest and strongest version of myself, and I visualize myself as such. This builds my self-esteem and my mind-body connection, helping me become more aware and in tune with myself.

At a very young age, I fell in love with the game of basketball, which ultimately led to my love and passion for being active and athletic. It's truly a joy to reap the results after training consistently. The results are not just about what I see, it's also about how I feel physically and mentally.

My fitness journey began with calisthenics, and as my journey continues, it is still a part of my regimen. I 100% recommend it for anyone who is looking to start their fitness journey and for those who are already going strong! Calisthenics is a form of exercise that involves using your body weight to perform various movements and exercises without the need for equipment or weights. It is a form of resistance training that can be done almost anywhere and anytime. Calisthenics can provide a full-body workout, helping you to build strength, endurance, flexibility, and agility. It is a great way for you to improve overall fitness, and it can be adapted to suit any fitness level, from beginner to advanced. My ultimate go-tos for a quick yet effective upper-body workout are push-ups, pull-ups, and dips. Between these three compound exercises, you will grow your chest, back, and arms. Each of these exercises targets different muscle groups, making them a great combination for a well-rounded upper-body workout.

After you get that intense workout in, you hydrate hydrate hydrate, and now you need to continue nourishing and nurturing your temple through rest, relaxation, and sound sleep.

Sleep is crucial for bodily repair and growth. It helps maintain proper immune function, supports growth and development in children and adolescents, and aids in tissue repair and muscle recovery. Adequate sleep is essential for optimal daily functioning, including work or school performance, decision-making, and creativity.

Hygiene

Personal hygiene is the cornerstone of maintaining good health. It involves maintaining the cleanliness of one's body, clothes, and surroundings to prevent the spread of germs, infections, and unpleasant odors. With the ever-growing risk of infectious diseases and the increasing awareness of public health, proper personal hygiene has become an essential aspect of daily life. Our skin is the largest organ and the first line of defense against infections. Regular bathing removes dirt, sweat, and dead skin cells that can harbor harmful bacteria. Using gentle soap and warm water helps cleanse the skin without causing irritation. Moisturizing after bathing helps maintain healthy, supple skin.

Good oral hygiene is essential for maintaining healthy teeth and gums, as well as preventing bad breath. Brushing teeth at least twice a day, flossing, and using mouthwash helps remove

"THE TEMPLE"

plaque and bacteria. Regular dental check-ups and cleanings ensure optimal oral health.

Hands are a primary vector for the spread of germs, making hand hygiene crucial for good health. Washing hands with soap and water or using hand sanitizer, especially before eating or preparing food, after using the restroom, and after touching potentially contaminated surfaces, can significantly reduce the risk of illness. Good hygiene is essential for maintaining a pleasant appearance and smell, which can impact how others perceive and interact with you.

A clean and well-groomed appearance will boost self-confidence and self-esteem. Personal hygiene practices will also serve as a form of self-care, promoting relaxation and stress relief.

We must eliminate and decrease stress as much as possible, as this is a key component in the well-being of our physical bodies. Stress can have negative effects on the body such as increased blood pressure, decreased immune function, and digestive issues, so we all must find ways to keep stress at a minimum. Some things that work for us are daily meditation, deep breathing exercises, and—as we already stated—training physically. Everyone should participate in regular physical exams, blood tests, and screenings for certain cancers and chronic diseases. Early detection and treatment of health issues can help to prevent complications and improve outcomes. One thing that we have noticed with men in general is that most procrastinate on getting themselves checked out on a regular basis. It is imperative that we all take the initiative to get with our personal provider on a routine check-up at least annually. What helps us remember is to schedule our check-ups sometime in our birth month.

6
"THE HAVES AND THE HAVE-NOTS"

First and foremost, we truly believe that the accumulation of wealth is the byproduct of getting in tune with ourselves spiritually, mentally, and physically. Our spirits, our minds, and our bodies are all priceless and should always be a top priority. Everything that is really worthwhile in life, we were born with. No amount of money can replace good health, happiness, and inner peace.

And that is why finance is the last of the Big Four (SMPF). After we come to the realization that we are spiritual beings having a human experience, understand how our mind literally shapes our destiny and destination, and nourish and nurture our one and only body, then last but not least, the final touch to living a balanced life full of love, peace, and prosperity the "SMPF" way is developing ourselves financially. Finances are a key component

"THE HAVES AND THE HAVE-NOTS"

of the lifestyle that you live. Life is what everyone has; style is how you live it.

Finances play a crucial role in determining the choices and opportunities available to you. It's important to remember that lifestyle is more than just your financial situation. It's about the way you live your life, including your values, interests, relationships, and experiences. By focusing on creating a fulfilling and meaningful lifestyle, rather than just accumulating wealth, you can find greater happiness and satisfaction, regardless of your financial situation. And by taking care of your finances and making informed decisions, you can create a solid foundation that allows you to live the life you want with greater freedom and abundance. You can create a lifestyle that aligns with your values, priorities, and aspirations. Money is a tool that, when used wisely, can facilitate personal growth, provide comfort and security, and enable us to make a difference in the world.

The lack of money is similar to claustrophobia. Financial struggles make it extremely difficult to move around freely how you please. You're confined in a tight space waiting for the next deposit to hit your bank account. On the other side, the brighter side, the abundance of money allows you to soar swiftly as an eagle. That abundance can give you greater freedom, flexibility, and the ability to truly live life on your own terms.

Timothy Trammer II:

Since I was a teenager in high school, I've always wanted the freedom, flexibility, and money to live life on my own terms. I wasn't a fan of waking up at six in the morning Monday through Friday, then being in school for eight hours. As I was in class, I would daydream about my future lifestyle. This lifestyle would consist of me waking up and going to sleep whenever I want to; traveling across the globe whenever I choose, knowing that I'd never have to worry about money ever again; being capable of blessing anyone at any time with a substantial amount of money. I can go on and on; however, the point is that this type of lifestyle isn't just handed out. For some time, I thought that life would be much easier once I got out of high school. I thought everything was just going to roll smoothly into this life that I used to ponder over in class. I quickly realized two things: this life that I envision for myself is 100% attainable, and I am more than capable of attaining much more. The real question is, what am I willing to do in order to live that balanced life full of love, peace, and prosperity? That is a question that I still ask myself to this day, and the answer always involves consistency, discipline, and intellectual curiosity. As I continue to grow, I have become aware that the majority of people aren't willing to be consistent, have discipline, or even be intellectually curious. If you struggle with these traits, you may find it tough to progress financially.

* * *

The world is slowly but surely splitting into two: the have-nots and the have-yachts.

"The haves and the have-nots" is a term used to describe a noticeable and significant economic difference between two groups of people. This dichotomy illustrates the divide between those who have access to resources and wealth (the haves) and those who do not (the have-nots). The definition of "dichotomy" is a division or contrast between two things that are presented

"THE HAVES AND THE HAVE-NOTS"

as opposites or entirely different. It often refers to a situation where two opposing elements or ideas are distinctly separate and do not overlap.

The "haves" typically refers to individuals or groups who are financially well off and possess substantial wealth, resources, or privileges. This can include material wealth such as property and money, as well as non-material advantages like access to quality education, healthcare, and opportunities for professional advancement. On the other hand, the "have-nots" typically refers to those who lack these resources or privileges. They may have lower incomes, fewer assets, less access to quality education or healthcare, and fewer opportunities for professional and social advancement.

We are not sure if you're a part of the "haves" or the "have-nots." But you should know if you're P.O.O.R.! That is an acronym for Passing On Opportunities Repeatedly. If the truth be told, we all have passed up on opportunities that could have taken our finances to another level. What holds people back from capitalizing on opportunities? Lack of knowledge, fear, and not knowing what an opportunity looks like.

Without sufficient information or understanding, people most likely will not recognize the potential of an opportunity or know how to capitalize on it. This is why continuous learning and personal development are essential for financial success. Fear of failure, rejection, losing funds, or the unknown can prevent people from taking risks or stepping out of their comfort zones. No risk, no reward! Overcoming fear involves building self-confidence, developing a growth mindset, and learning to embrace failures as opportunities for growth and learning.

"THE HAVES AND THE HAVE-NOTS"

Some people may not be able to identify opportunities because they are not actively seeking them, they are too focused on their current situation, or they lack the imagination and creativity to see potential in new ideas or situations. Cultivating a curious and open mindset, staying informed about trends and developments in various fields, and networking with diverse groups of people will help in recognizing opportunities. Delaying or postponing action can cause people to miss out on valuable opportunities. Overcoming procrastination involves setting clear goals to accomplish daily, breaking tasks into manageable steps, and cultivating discipline and learning to invest your time wisely. Sometimes, people may have difficulty capitalizing on opportunities due to a lack of financial resources, time, or other necessary assets. In these cases, it's essential to prioritize and allocate resources strategically, seek outside help, or explore creative solutions to overcome limitations.

A lack of belief in one's abilities or worth can make it difficult for people to pursue opportunities or take risks. Overcoming self-doubt involves building self-esteem, setting realistic expectations, and learning to accept and appreciate one's strengths and weaknesses.

We have no clue if you are Passing On Opportunities Repeatedly (P.O.O.R.). That's between you and you. One thing we are sure of is that the choices and investments you make today in terms of time, energy, and money will have a significant impact on your life in the future. It's crucial to be intentional and strategic in how you allocate these resources in order to create the life you desire. There is an abundance of financial growth opportunities! No lack whatsoever! Never has there been, and there certainly never will be. In today's age and moving forward, you cannot

"THE HAVES AND THE HAVE-NOTS"

deny the fact that the opportunities are abundant and limitless. Either embrace it or let it pass you by.

Money is a necessity that makes the world spin. Everyone's perspective and perception of money is different. Money is a medium of exchange that facilitates transactions of goods and services between people. It serves as a store of value, a unit of account, and a means of payment. Throughout history, money has taken many different forms, including physical objects like shells, precious metals, and paper currency, as well as digital currencies like Bitcoin and Ethereum. People's perceptions of money can be influenced by a variety of factors, including their upbringing, cultural background, socioeconomic status, and personal experiences. For some people, money may represent security, freedom, and opportunity, while for others, it may be associated with greed, corruption, and inequality. People have different attitudes towards earning, spending, and saving money based on their personal values and priorities. Money plays a significant role in the functioning of modern societies. It's important to recognize that your individual perspective and perception of money will ultimately have a profound impact on your life and the world around you.

Let's say that there are two people, one who is considered a "have" and the other a "have-not." The "have" is a wealthy individual who inherited a large sum of money from their family and has never had to worry about finances. The "have-not" is someone who grew up in poverty and has struggled to make ends meet their entire life.

From the perspective of the "have," money may be seen as a means to achieve their goals and desires. They may view money as a tool that allows them to live a comfortable and enjoyable life, to travel to exotic places, to buy expensive cars or houses, or to invest in businesses that generate more wealth. Money may be seen as a source of power and status, and having a lot of it may be perceived as a measure of success and accomplishment.

On the other hand, from the perspective of the "have-not," money may be seen as a source of stress and anxiety. They may view money as a constant struggle, something that they never have enough of to cover their basic needs, such as food, shelter, and healthcare. Money may be seen as a barrier that prevents them from pursuing their dreams and goals, and as a result, they may feel powerless and trapped in their situation. They may also perceive the "haves" as privileged and out of touch with the struggles of the working class. Clearly, the perspective on money will differ between the haves and the have-nots, with the haves seeing it as a means to achieve their goals and desires, and the have-nots seeing it as a source of stress and inequality. If you live in America, there is no lack or scarcity financially, regardless of whether you are financially well off and never have to worry about money again, or you are in the middle where you live comfortably but are not wealthy, or you are living paycheck to paycheck and barely making ends meet.

Taking ownership of one's finances and preparing economically is crucial to achieving financial freedom and security. Conversely, being nonchalant about your financial well-being may result in financial struggles and limited opportunities, which will lead to other stresses and negative outcomes. Financial freedom and security is something that the majority of people would sleep

"THE HAVES AND THE HAVE-NOTS"

more peacefully at night if they had. Proactively managing your money, investing wisely, and planning for the future will lead to a lifestyle where money is no longer a source of stress or constraint.

With that being said, your perception and perspective of money must shift first—shift towards abundance, prosperity, and limitless possibilities, even if your bank account, savings account, and credit cards say otherwise. Becoming a multimillionaire and creating wealth is not about putting money on a pedestal and "chasing a bag" as some would call it.

As Bob Proctor wrote in It's Not About the Money, "Your mind is the most powerful wealth creation tool that exists. It doesn't matter who you are. It doesn't matter what you've done up till now. Everytime you think of money and wealth, think of all the positives associated with them." Visualize yourself being a lender and not a borrower. See yourself in your mind giving generously to your family members. Envision yourself blessing people financially to the point that their life is forever changed.

While having a large amount of money can certainly provide financial security and freedom, the process of building wealth often starts with a change in mindset and attitude towards money. This includes developing a positive and abundant mindset, setting clear financial goals, being disciplined with your spending and saving, and seeking out opportunities for growth and investment. It also means being mindful of your financial habits and making informed decisions, rather than simply chasing after money for its own sake. By focusing on building a strong financial foundation and adopting a holistic approach to your finances, you can create a path to wealth and financial prosperity that is sustainable and fulfilling.

7
"DON'T LET YOUR MONEY $TOP"

In this chapter, we will discuss why in today's society and going forward it is vital to have multiple sources of income and not to let your money stop. We will also discuss four levels of providing value and how this can lead to keeping your funds flowing. Last but not least, we will reveal various ways to invest your time, energy, and money wisely so you can live a balanced life full of love, peace, and prosperity.

In today's fast-paced and ever-evolving world, financial stability has become an essential aspect of life. The average person has only one source of income, which is typically their full-time job. At the average full-time job, most employees are paid either weekly or biweekly based upon the hourly rate or salary that was set in the terms. Once this person clocks out or is done with their shift, regardless of the hourly rate or salary, their money stops immediately. When we say "their money stops," this means that the employee is no longer earning money from that source of income until they clock back in or begin the next shift. It is definitely a blessing to have any source of income in the first place; however, one is too close to none.

In today's ever-changing economic landscape, financial stability is a significant concern for individuals and families. With rising living costs, job insecurity, and fluctuating markets, relying on a single source of income is beyond risky. We all have experienced an unexpected job loss and incurred unexpected expenses—or, if not, then we all have witnessed someone else experience this. Dependence on a single stream often doesn't allow for significant growth in income or financial flexibility.

Ask yourself this: Am I ready for significant growth in my bank account, savings account, and investment portfolio, and to have overall financial flexibility? If your answer is "Yes, an increase in those areas would be great," then keeping your money in motion and having multiple streams is the most logical solution. The journey to financial freedom requires diligence and a well-crafted strategy. Ensuring that your money is consistently working for you is a crucial aspect of financial success. When you rely solely on a single source of income, such as a full-time job, you are left vulnerable to financial hardships and stress, which ultimately limits your overall financial potential and makes it challenging to achieve financial freedom. Having only one source of income is tough enough, but when you are trading your time for money, this can add more constraint, especially if your time is not invested wisely when you are off the clock. One of the primary disadvantages of trading time for money is the inherent limitation on earning potential. The number of hours one can work in a day is limited, and as a result, the amount of money earned through this method is also limited.

Knowing that your money is capped when you are at an hourly or salaried job, you must manage, maximize, and multiply your money strategically if you desire to advance economically. Creating a detailed budget is the first step towards effective money management. By tracking income and expenses, individuals can identify areas where they can reduce costs and allocate more funds towards saving, investing, and debt repayment. Living below one's means and cutting unnecessary expenses can help maximize the money available for wealth-building activities. If you find yourself in a restricted financial situation, then embracing a frugal lifestyle and living below your means is a wise option instead of trying to "keep up with the Joneses." This phrase refers to the tendency of individuals to compare their social status, material possessions, and lifestyle to those of their peers, often striving to match or surpass them. This phenomenon can lead to a never-ending pursuit of materialistic goals, driven by the desire to maintain a certain image and social standing. While it may seem harmless on the surface, this mindset can have significant negative consequences on one's financial well-being, mental health, and overall life satisfaction.

Maximizing one's main source of income can be achieved through various strategies that focus on enhancing skills, increasing productivity, and seeking opportunities for advancement. By investing time and effort in personal and professional growth, individuals can increase their earning potential and make the most of their primary income source. Invest in yourself by seeking opportunities to learn and grow professionally. This may involve taking courses, attending workshops, or acquiring certifications relevant to your field. By enhancing your skills, you can increase your value to your employer and make yourself eligible for promotions, raises, or higher-paying job opportunities.

When you demonstrate a strong work ethic by being on time, reliable, and committed to your job, this can help you stand out as a valuable employee. By consistently meeting or exceeding expectations, you can position yourself for advancement within your organization. Cultivating strong professional relationships with colleagues, supervisors, and other individuals in your field can open doors to new opportunities and help you stay informed about potential job openings, promotions, or projects. We recommend you attend networking events, join professional associations, and engage with people on social media to expand your network. Keep up to date with developments in your field to ensure that your skills and knowledge remain relevant. This can help you identify new opportunities for growth and advancement, as well as potential threats to your job security. Volunteer for new projects or additional responsibilities at work that showcase your skills and dedication. By demonstrating your ability to handle more complex tasks, you can prove your worth and make a case for a salary increase, promotion, or bonus.

Now that you are managing your funds effectively and maximizing your main source of income, it is time to get that money in motion. The importance of having multiple sources of income and not allowing your money to stop cannot be overstated. By diversifying income streams, you will achieve greater financial stability, increase your earning potential, and accelerate the wealth-building process.

"DON'T LET YOUR MONEY STOP"

We (Timothy Trammer I and Timothy Trammer II) sat around the round table to brainstorm and strategize a blueprint that we have put together, which involves us passing down generational wealth to anyone who is born into the Trammer family. Proverbs 13:22 (NKJV) states, "A good man leaves an inheritance to his children's children." This verse keeps our life goals, our vision, and our legacy front and center when we're choosing how to use our money today. When we weigh what we want now against what we really want later, we realize how the desire for temporary satisfaction shrinks in comparison to a legacy of purpose and generational fulfillment.

Leaving an inheritance is certainly not limited to money. It can and should include intellectual property and "basic instructions before leaving earth" (BIBLE). That is exactly what we plan to pass down along with real estate, land, digital assets, and numerous books about how to Live a Balanced Life: The "SMPF" Way. Easier said than done, though. We must diversify our income and be mindful of how we invest our time, energy, and money. For starters, as this sentence is being written, we are currently generating revenue from a few streams, including but not limited to real estate, transportation/logistics, and blockchain technology. These are three industries that will continue to thrive and increase in opportunities for the rest of your lifetime.

Great news—we live in a land and a time where the opportunities to create wealth and have abundance are totally up to you. Like we said before, there is no lack, no scarcity whatsoever, especially since the Creator of all things gave us all a prominent quality that He possesses, which is the capability to create. Everything that is currently around us day by day is a creation that was first created in the mind of a powerful human, then manifested in the physical form. We have done just that! This book was first an idea in the back of our mind, and now you have access to it just how we envisioned it. As we search for more ways to keep our funds flowing, we must keep in mind that, as Kenneth Burke wrote, "Money follows value like a dog on a leash. Where you continually find value, there you will find people willing to (quite literally) hand over their money. If you're doing well, helping others, and providing real value to lives and communities, you will gain a reputation as one worth working with."

As a business or individual, when you create more value, you attract more wealth. If you merely exchange your time for money (like in a traditional job), you are limited by the hours you can work. But if you create a product, service, or system that provides value to people even when you're not actively working on it, you can generate income continually. That is one of the reasons why we created this book. We wrote this after becoming aware of ourselves and our surroundings and noticing that the majority of society is living a life of uncertainty and no direction, which leads to an unbalanced life. As we continue to develop and progress spiritually, mentally, physically, and financially, it is of great value for us to share this intellectual property—not only to share it with our immediate family but to spread it to the masses as well. Anyone can easily get access to this value by purchasing a physical copy of the book, audio version, and/or ebook. These are three ways of generating revenue from only one creation, and this creation will outlive us.

"DON'T LET YOUR MONEY $TOP"

Levels of Value

As you are actively searching for ways to keep your money in motion and generate revenue, you must understand the levels of value, because money follows value. Understanding these levels of value will help guide you in strategizing your wealth-building. You should aim to build and offer higher levels of value, which can command more money and build multiple revenue streams, hence keeping your money in motion.

There are four main levels of value: 1) Implementation, 2) Unification, 3) Communication, and 4) Imagination. If you don't align perfectly with any one of these categories, that's not uncommon. In fact, numerous individuals often straddle multiple levels simultaneously. As we go deeper into the details of these stages, take a pause to consider your current position. Then, let your imagination take flight and envision your desired destination. Keep in mind, the key to progressing to the next level is straightforward: to level up, add more value to more people's lives.

Level 1 for providing value is Implementation. In this level, you're the individual carrying out the tasks—those at this level, referred to as Implementers, are the ones who physically accomplish the work. Whether it's being a mechanic at an auto shop, a cook at a restaurant, a housekeeper, or any other task, you're the one doing the physical labor. Every hotel establishment is supported by a dedicated team of housekeeping personnel. These individuals carry out some of the most physically demanding tasks within the hotel, ensuring that the premises are clean, comfortable, and welcoming for the guests. Despite the importance and strenuous labor, the housekeepers are paid the least out of all of the hotel employees, simply because they are the implementers.

Even though Level 1 presents its own inherent value through the completion of tasks and hands-on work, it comes with a significant limitation. You are most likely using your muscles over time, and muscles are a physical resource, while time is a limited resource. The constraint of time becomes a significant drawback because your earnings are directly proportional to the number of hours you dedicate to work. Essentially, you're trading your time for money, which means your potential to generate value is cut short by the number of hours available in a day. This structure most definitely limits your earning potential because, after all, there's a maximum limit to the number of hours you can work in a day, and thus a ceiling to the amount of income you can generate in a day. It is extremely difficult to prosper using a physical resource and a limited resource as your only source of income.

An essential aspect of elevating your earnings involves situating yourself within Level 2, the Unification level. By transitioning more facets of your personal brand and or business to embrace the "Level 2 mindset," you can significantly expand your impact. At this level, your most valuable asset for generating income lies in your management and leadership skills. In Level 2, your main role is to oversee and direct the individuals who are responsible for carrying out the tasks.

In the Unification level, the emphasis is less on performing the tasks yourself and more on managing those who do. Your role evolves from a doer to a director, overseeing and guiding those who execute the tasks. It involves a shift from direct involvement to a more strategic role, where your decisions and directions influence a larger outcome. Your primary tool for generating income at this level is not your ability to perform tasks, but your management and leadership skills. You're no longer limited by the hours you can work. Instead, your income potential is multiplied by the number of people you manage and the efficiency with which you can guide them. It doesn't matter if you're managing a Taco Bell or a Rolls Royce dealership, moving into the management leadership role is always an increase in income compared to those who are the Implementers.

Furthermore, in Level 2, you have the opportunity to develop and refine these leadership skills. This level allows you to broaden your horizons, gain new insights, and grow as a leader. It's about learning how to delegate effectively, motivate your team, and make strategic decisions that enhance productivity and efficiency. By embracing the Unification level, you're improving not just your income potential, but also your professional growth and personal development. It's an exciting journey that can lead to a rewarding career and a more significant impact on your field.

Transitioning into this new level begins with a simple exercise: identify and jot down your most preferred aspect of your work. What is that single most essential task or "number one skill" that you excel at? Following that, list all the other tasks associated with running your business or daily duties at your job that distract you or prevent you from focusing on your core skills. Start contemplating whether you could potentially reach and serve a larger audience with your primary skill if you delegated some of those additional tasks. It's possible that your "number one skill" still falls within the Implementation level, and that's perfectly fine.

The key is to free up as much of your time as possible for your core competency by outsourcing the rest. By doing so, you can enhance your efficiency and proficiency at your primary task, thereby delivering better and faster results. This in turn enables you to reach and benefit more people, which essentially means you've leveled up. Remember, the idea is not to do everything but to do what you do best and delegate the rest. This shift towards focusing on your strengths and delegating other tasks is a strategic move that not only elevates your work and financial position but also increases your personal productivity and job satisfaction. This is an essential step towards growth and scaling your operations. It's about working smarter, not harder, and making the most of your unique skills and talents.

At Level 3, Communication, your verbal abilities become the cornerstone of wealth generation. There are two requirements for this level: a mouth and the competence to use it precisely. Myron Golden once said, "You must learn how to have conversations that create cash flow. You need to know how to develop and deliver a message that moves the masses. At this level, you want to start using better words and get better at using words." While you may not necessarily be an actor, musician, or orator, your primary asset in this stage is your communicative ability. This level revolves around the concept of using communication as a tool not only to amplify your income but also to provide value to others. In this context, the term "voice" transcends its literal meaning. It's not limited to spoken words but includes all forms of communication, be it written, visual, or even non-verbal cues. It's about effectively transmitting your thoughts, ideas, or information in a manner that resonates with your audience, compels action, or incites change.

"DON'T LET YOUR MONEY STOP"

The ability to communicate effectively, with clarity and persuasion, can be a powerful tool for wealth creation. Whether it's through writing compelling content, delivering captivating speeches, or using visual storytelling, your voice can be a medium to influence, inspire, and educate. It can help you build a personal brand, establish authority in your field, or sell products or services. At the same time, using your voice effectively is not just about earning more income for yourself. It's equally about contributing positively to others' lives. It's about sharing knowledge, sparking innovation, fostering understanding, and encouraging progress. Whether you're helping your team to work more effectively, guiding your customers to make informed decisions, or inspiring your audience to achieve their potential, your voice can be a catalyst for positive change. So, in Level 3, the focus shifts from merely managing resources to harnessing the power of communication. It's about using your voice strategically to create value, influence outcomes, and ultimately generate wealth. This is a level where your words become your wealth.

Your mind and your intellect are your most valuable assets in wealth creation. Individuals at Level 4, Imagination, are the visionaries, those who consistently find ways to improve the quality of life for all. They are the dream-catchers, those with a unique ability to envision and actualize ideas that others may consider improbable or impossible. These are the people who don't just think outside the box; they redefine the box. They hold the power to instigate transformative changes, altering the foundational structures of entire industries. One doesn't need to be an iconic figure like Steve Jobs, Walt Disney, or Oprah Winfrey to operate at Level 4. The mindset characteristic of Level 4 can be incorporated into any business, regardless of its nature or size. Operating at the Imagination level will lead to remarkable innovations and breakthroughs, driving growth and prosperity in your business and beyond. "You can use words without thinking, but you cannot think without using words." The Communication and Imagination levels are well connected. These are the two highest levels of value and wealth creation when used intentionally, and they are the ones that we (Timothy Trammer I and Timothy Trammer II) are becoming well familiar with. We understand that our words, thoughts, and actions all must align.

Where are your current and desired destinations out of these four stages? Remember that the secret to leveling up is simple: to level up, add more value to more people's lives.

Invest Time, Energy, and Money

Investing wisely is an art and a discipline that extends beyond the realm of finance. It is a holistic concept that permeates every aspect of our lives, from the way we manage our time and energy to how we nurture our relationships and personal growth. Invest your time in activities that energize you and align with your goals, use your energy on tasks that yield the highest return, and invest your money in ways that provide security and growth. This approach ensures that your resources are not only preserved but also multiplied. This form of investment involves conscious decision-making, strategic planning, and an understanding of the value of our resources. Whether it's the precious hours we have in a day, the energy that fuels our productivity, or the financial resources at our disposal, each deserves mindful stewardship. Furthermore, wise investment is not just about conservation but also about growth. It's about making choices that not only preserve our resources but also enhance them. It's also about recognizing that every minute, every ounce of energy, and every penny you possess can be a seed, and if planted and cared for correctly, it can grow into something much greater. The ultimate goal is to create a cycle of sustainable growth that enriches our lives and the lives of those around us.

Wealth, prosperity, and abundance are the byproducts of us first getting in tune with ourselves spiritually, mentally, and physically. Once we are in alignment with ourselves in these ways, we will know and understand where to invest our time, energy, and money. That's why we start with spiritual alignment, since this involves being in tune with God, our inner selves, and the universe at large. It's about understanding our purpose in life, our values, and our passions. It's a journey of self-discovery and introspection that guides us towards our true calling. When we are spiritually aligned, we are better able to discern where to direct our energy, how to spend our time, and what causes or ventures to invest our well-earned income into. Our decisions are driven not only by financial gain, but also by a deeper sense of purpose and fulfillment.

Mental alignment, on the other hand, involves having a clear and focused mind. It's about nurturing a positive mindset, cultivating resilience, and continuously learning and growing. A mentally attuned individual is capable of making sound decisions; overcoming challenges; and navigating the complexities of life with wisdom, serenity, and grace. This mental clarity and resilience is crucial in managing our time, energy, and money effectively.

Physical alignment is about maintaining a healthy and active lifestyle. It's about understanding and respecting the intimate connection between our physical health and our overall well-being and productivity. When we are physically aligned, we have the energy and vitality needed to pursue our goals and dreams. This physical well-being directly impacts our ability to manage our time and energy efficiently and to make wise financial decisions. Once we are attuned to these aspects of ourselves, we gain the clarity and wisdom to invest our time, energy, and money in ways that others who are not attuned the "SMPF" way cannot.

In conclusion, understanding and implementing the art of investing time, energy, and money wisely is not just a process; it's a transformative journey of personal growth and self-discovery. It requires discipline, patience, and continuous learning, necessitating a commitment to introspection, evolution, and the cultivation of wisdom. This journey may pose challenges and demand sacrifices, but the growth and understanding that come from navigating these challenges make the journey itself immensely rewarding. The rewards extend beyond tangible outcomes like success and financial freedom. They seep into every facet of life, leading to personal fulfillment, a sense of purpose, and a profound understanding of oneself and the world. Moreover, this journey imbues life with a richness that goes beyond material wealth. It helps us foster deep connections with ourselves and others, creating a life that resonates with our deepest values and aspirations. It allows us to become architects of our destiny, shaping our future with intention and purpose.

So, embark on this journey with an open heart and a willing spirit. Harness the discipline to invest your time, the patience to manage your energy, and the wisdom to allocate your money. The path may be long, and the climb may be steep, but the view from the top—a life of fulfillment, success, and financial freedom—is an unparalleled reward that validates every ounce of effort expended. Bear in mind, each stride made on this path of growth and understanding, no matter how small or incremental, brings you one step closer to the life you have envisioned for yourself—a life marked by accomplishment, prosperity, and personal satisfaction. Always remember, your progress, like a journey, is not solely about the destination, but about appreciating and learning from each step along the way.

"DON'T LET YOUR MONEY $TOP"

www.ingramcontent.com/pod-product-compliance
Lightning Source LLC
Chambersburg PA
CBHW071202090426
42736CB00012B/2421